Black Sea, Golden Steppes

ACKNOWLEDGMENTS

Joseph Marshall, the eighteenth-century author, commenting on Ukraine in volume 3 of his *Travels*, noted that "the country's being so extremely out of the way of all travellers, not a person in a century goes to it, who takes notes of his observations with intentions to lay them before the world ..." Happily, Marshall was wrong. In returning to the study of maps of Ukraine and Eastern Europe more generally, I am quietly surprised by how much there is to see both in the way of observations as well as the silences. This excites one's curiosity and it is perhaps for this reason that my passion for cartography is so easily rekindled. Luckily, I am not alone in my enthusiasm, several individuals kindly offering assistance at various stages of the project: Murray and Lissa Gruza, Alec Parley, Michael Dowler, and especially Kent Archer of the Kenderdine Gallery, University of Saskatchewan, for agreeing to host the exhibit. Additionally, Edison del Canto, whose appreciable talents were applied in the design of the publication, deserves special mention, as does Ron Curtis for his skilful editing of the final draft of the manuscript. Finally, I would be remiss if I failed to acknowledge Danya who has cheerfully endured my whimsical excesses and Christian for joyfully helping me to find my magnifying glass.

In association with the
Prairie Centre for the Study of Ukrainian Heritage
and Kenderdine Art Gallery

National Library of Canada Cataloguing in Publication Data

Kordan, Bohdan S.
 Black Sea, Golden Steppes

 Co-published by: Prairie Centre for the Study of Ukrainian Heritage and Kenderdine Gallery
 ISBN 0-88880-448-2

 1. Black Sea Region—Historical geography—Maps. 2. Crimea (Ukraine)—Historical geography
 —Maps. 3. Ukraine—Historical geography—Maps. I. Prairie Centre for the Study of Ukrainian
 Heritage. II Kenderdine Art Gallery. III. Title
G1782.B5K67 2001   912'.196389   C2001-911146-0

Heritage Press   2001
Prairie Centre for the Study of Ukrainian Heritage
St. Thomas More College
University of Saskatchewan
Saskatoon, Saskatchewan
Canada   S7N 0W6

This publication was made possible in part through a grant from
DR. VICTOR BUYNIAK

Designed by Edison del Canto Design
Printed by Houghton Boston

CONTENTS

Black Sea, Golden Steppes

ANTIQUARIAN MAPS
of the Black Sea Coast and the Steppes of Old Ukraine

Bohdan S. KORDAN

Heritage Press

INTRODUCTION

The word *Ukrania* – Ukraine – has been interpreted to mean frontier in various senses, not all of them geographic. Appearing early on in such accounts as the twelfth-century *Primary Chronicle* (*Povest vremennykh let*), *Ukrania* would come into its own during the Renaissance. Usage follows appropriateness, and no word would more aptly capture the fate that had befallen the lands once embraced by the mediaeval polity of Kyivan-Rus'. Dynastic conflict (during the eleventh and twelfth centuries) and Mongol invasion (the thirteenth century), as well as the influence of the Mongol Golden Horde and the Crimean Khanate (the fourteenth and fifteenth centuries), and still later the Ottoman hegemony (the sixteenth and seventeenth centuries) would all serve to radically alter political developments in the region, as well as the landscape. In the fifteenth century, for example, the territory, diminished in importance and peripheralized in status, would sustain all but a primitive political economy, one that relied on closed trade in several commodities, principally fur and spices, and silks and slaves to be sold in the Venetian and Genoese ports at Tana on the Sea of Azov and Kaffa and Cembalo in the Crimea. Caught in this unfavourable situation, Ukraine was truly a frontier.

Ukraine, however, was a frontier in more ways than one. There was, to be sure, the geographic divide brought about by population loss that had been fed by conflict, especially as European interest in the form of the expanding Grand Duchy of Lithuania and, later, the Polish-Lithuanian Commonwealth, challenged for control the waning power of the Golden Horde and subsequently the might of the Ottoman Turk. The long, steady demographic decline, as well as the regional contest, which was culturally rooted in religion, would result in the land's reputation as being uninhabited, or *Dzike Pole* – the Wild Fields. The Pontic Steppe, however, was much more than *loca deserta*, as it was commonly described in sixteenth- and seventeenth-century maps. That it appeared to be deserted was the evidence needed to support a mental construct, one that represented in the European mind – from the Renaissance onwards, or at least until the period of the Enlightenment – an allegory for binary opposites: the difference between the known and the unknown, civilization and barbarism, Christianity and Islam, Europe and Asia, order and chaos.

The conceptual role that Ukraine would play derived from the modern European preoccupation with defining itself in civilizational terms. In the face of growing cultural contact with the external world and because of an ideological need to rationalize European rapine, the quest for identity would lead to a psychology of contrasts. If Eastern Europe, as the historian Larry Wolff has so brilliantly argued, would help by way of "opposites" to define what it meant to be civilized – and therefore part of Europe – then Ukraine was clearly the proving ground. As it was for their ancient predecessors Herodotus and Strabo, so it was for such "modern" European luminaries as Voltaire, Gibbon, and Adam Smith that here, in the nether world, at Europe's furthest reach, civilization stopped. That information on Ukraine was scarce made it all the more attractive as a point of reference.

Not surprisingly, Ukraine would take on a mythic quality, deriving from impressions largely predicated on ancient stories and half-truths. Greek myths and Christian legend, along with spurious information from traders and travellers alike – especially those who had never visited – all combined to create a place as much imagined as it was real. It was here, for instance, that the she-warrior Amazons were said to have dwelt. But more especially it was here that Herodotus' original barbarians, the Scythians, made their home, and it was from here that subsequent barbaric tribes, the Goths and the Huns, would surface in their westward push. It was here also that the Sarmatians, Alans, Antes, Bulgarians, Slavs, and others – barbarians or semibarbarians all – reproduced to threaten civilization. That the territory should later become home to the Mongol-Tatars and the brigand Zaporozhian Cossacks – "the strangest people who are on the earth," according to Voltaire – seemed altogether fitting.

But the potential of Ukraine was also part of this cultural narrative. Descriptions of Ukraine would abound, some more fanciful than others. Universally, however, they spoke temptingly of the natural bounty of the land. That it was wasted on the local inhabitants was a given. Ukraine was rich, and the rewards were great. But with rewards came risk. For those who would venture into these unfamiliar lands – whether Darius I, the would-be conqueror of the Scythians, or Charles XII, in his bid to make Sweden the preeminent European power some twenty-two hundred years later – Ukraine, prophetically, would be their undoing.

Critically, maps, those ideational representations of space, or as J. B. Harley argues, those "socially constructed perspectives on the world," would incorporate the basic elements of this cultural narrative. The ancient maps of Ptolemy, for instance, would be reproduced by Mercator, Jansson, and others in the sixteenth and seventeenth centuries, ostensibly for historical interest but also because they provided a familiar, if not comfortable, perspective on Europe. The borders of "modern" Europe coincided with the ancient understanding of civilization, the Tanais, or Don, River, demarcating Europe from Asia. To underscore the point, geographic atlases of world history produced in the late seventeenth and early eighteenth centuries – the atlases of Cluver and Mallet, for example – unquestioningly repeated the observation that Saramtia had both a European and an Asian face and that European Sarmatia went no further than the Don. Europe, in effect, ended in *Ukrania* – the borderlands – but just.

Indeed, conceptually Ukraine posed something of a problem. If the territory was European, then how was the presence of the Tatars of the Crimean Khanate to be explained, let alone countenanced? Through an intellectual sleight of hand, the problem was resolved at a certain level by simply rationalizing the existence of a European Tatary. The Crimean, Budziak and Nogay Tatars of the Black Sea steppes, while described as an obviously inferior race, were also portrayed as possessing certain admirable traits – notably courage – and in this way they were differentiated from the peoples of Asiatic Tatary. And yet from the perspective of religious ideology and the chasm that existed between Christianity and Islam, this was not an entirely satisfactory response. The larger question of civilization, coinciding as it did with the question of Europe's natural frontiers, demanded a more robust explanation.

The answer, of course, was that the borderland of Ukraine was in the process of becoming civilized. This answer, however, had a very precise meaning. Civilization was an unmistakably political affair, achieved when the familiar replaced the unfamiliar and order had been imposed on the chaos. It usually arrived in the form of the musket, the sabre, and the cannon. Power, in essence, would determine whether the borderlands would become part of European civilization, while annexation would be its seal.

Cartography as it would relate to the Crimea and the southern steppes of Ukraine from the sixteenth through to the eighteenth centuries was caught up in recording the contest for political power, the shifting fortunes of the many players, and the inexorable course of territorial conquest. There were at first the important maps of Waldseemüller, Ortelius, Mercator, Münster, and others in the mid- to late-sixteenth century, maps which documented the range of Lithuanian, Polish, and Muscovite influence. They were followed in the early seventeenth century by the exquisite maps of Blaeu describing European settlement along the frontier and the phenomenon of Cossack society at Europe's outpost, the *sich* beyond the treacherous cataracts (*za porohamy/za porogi*) of the timeless Borysthenes. To the extent that the Cossacks of Ukraine were able to organize an administrative structure, the new Cossack polity was recognized in the cartographic record. That it was short-lived (1649–57), however, meant that maps of the Cossack state, such as those produced by Jansson, Homman, and Seutter, were rare. It was not until Muscovy emerged as a power in its own right, after the Great Northern War (1700–21), that European cartography, narrating Russia's relentless pursuit of empire, would finally offer something other than a proximate political and geographic perspective on the region.

That more comprehensive and exact information on the Black Sea and on Crimea and the southern steppes of Ukraine was unavailable, at least before the Russian advance, had as much to do with the restricted use of maps in the Ottoman Empire as it did with the fact that the territory was largely inaccessible, except to the most adventurous. Based on earlier Italian reports and others as well, charts outlining the coast and coastal settlements were, of course, available, but in terms of chorography and topogra-

phy there was precious little data. Maps of the region, consequently, were impressionistic and often contradictory. The shape of the Crimean peninsula – trapezoidal or round – would, for example, remain a matter of contention for some time.

Accordingly, publishers would strain to acquire up-to-date information, which resulted in the recurring practice of borrowing and reworking material from competitors. The production of these composite maps, which would appear with astonishing frequency, was spurred on by a small but growing market for such items, especially among Europe's expanding commercial class. Luxurious atlases containing handsome images designed by Europe's premier illustrators and engravers lent cachet and helped fill ready-made libraries. But production was also stimulated, as was evident in the proliferation of small pocket atlases, by a growing carto-literacy and curiosity about the world, including reports of conflicts between Cossacks, Poles, Russians, Tatars, and Turks in the unknown lands to the east. And yet the commercial ability to produce maps with the accuracy demanded by a buying public was simply not there. In 1769 Joseph Marshall, a travel writer, was led, for instance, to conclude that the state of knowledge on Ukraine was seriously deficient after he had observed that recent maps that showed Right Bank Ukraine to be in the possession of Poland were at odds with news that the very same lands were now part of Russia and had been for some time. Marshall, in a clear moment of understatement, noted in passing that "the greatest changes happen in such remote parts of the world, without any thing of the matter being known." And yet, remarkably, he was speaking not of far-off America, with which he was familiar, but of Europe's doorstep, Ukraine.

The publishers' appetite for information based on the newest scientific observations paralleled the intense desire of European sovereigns to possess an accurate account of the lands they administered. The maturing Westphalian state system, with its emphasis on clearly delineated borders, provided a powerful incentive for sovereigns to support the enterprise of cartography. To know where resources might be harnessed in defence of the state and to establish and convey territorial sovereignty, both politically and diplomatically, became a paramount consideration for states in the eighteenth century. Frontiers, however, were not easily mediated, especially where empires were concerned. Consequently, for Russia's ambitious tsar, Peter I, as for the equally driven Catherine II, knowledge of the empire was as important as the military campaigns conducted in the gathering of the lands. Accordingly, state support for survey expeditions, both military and scientific, and the creation of a school of cartography became pivotal factors in Russian map-making. The result was the Russian Atlas of 1745, a massive undertaking and a high-point in Russian cartography – but also a product of imperial Russia's concerted effort to create and possess an image of itself.

Not surprisingly, the role of Russian state cartography in relation to the territory of Ukraine was very specific. There was, to be sure, the fact-finding dimension, but deeper still was the legitimizing aspect. With Poland's initial partition in 1772 and Russia's victories over the Ottoman Porte in several decisive wars (1739–45 and 1769–74), the newly acquired lands would be claimed as part of Europe – but under Russian favour. Russia's right to territory was reaffirmed not only through the reorganization and administration of the locale but also by its commission to renew. This would necessarily start with toponymy, since Tatar and Ukrainian place-names, of regions and settlements alike, were quickly replaced with imperial Russian designations.

As the hold of one empire over the land was replaced by another and as the last vestiges of Ukrainian Cossack autonomy and Crimean Tartar independence were abolished by the centralizing power of the Russian imperial state, a process completed in the 1780s, the language of appropriation used in asserting sovereign claim over the territory entered the vocabulary of European mapmakers and publishers – Vaugondy, Bellin, and Rizzi-Zannoni. Although it was to be expected, that it should have occurred so quickly and easily was unusual. Trying to make sense of what was only nominally familiar, where only historical anachronisms seemed to exist, European cartography borrowed directly from the Russian imperial scheme of provinces – the *namestnichestva*. In creating order out of chaos, this ready template was useful. But perhaps more to the point, it served a deeper need. From the perspective of European geography, the process of possessing a complete image of Europe – one that wrestled historically with the question of where and how Ukraine might fit – was finally concluded.

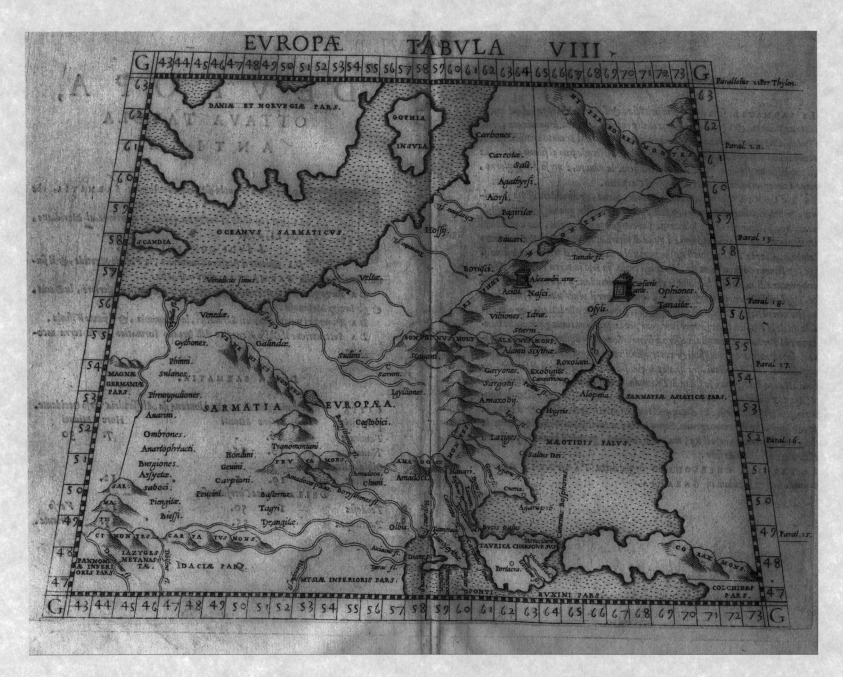

G. Gastaldi/ G. Ruscelli, *Europæ Tabula VIII* (1564)

T he fifteenth century – a transitional century – witnessed extraordinary developments that would set history on a different course. Mediaeval features and practices would be replaced by the drive to acquire a new understanding of both the world and man, while new geographic and scientific discoveries made it possible, according to Jacob Burkhardt, to say for the first time: 'il mondo è poco' – the world is small. But discovery did not necessarily imply acceptance. On the contrary, as cultures came in contact, suspicion often accompanied the impulse to know. In particular, to the east, that is to say, beyond the Vistula, the abstracted idea of Europe would not ordinarily apply, certainly not before the mid-sixteenth century, for it was here that Herodotus' original barbarians, the Scythians and,

G. Gastaldi/ G. Ruscelli, *Europæ Tabula VIII* (1564)
S. Münster, *Tartaria, Moscovia* (c.1565)
S. Münster, *Sarmatia Europæ* (c. 1592)
M. Quadt, *Polonia (1594)*
A. Jenkinson/A. Ortelius, *Russiæ, Moscoviæ, Tartariæ* (1598)

later, the Sarmatians resided. Yet the Black Sea was part of the maritime world of the classical Greeks and Romans, and it was thus civilization: to dismiss it as being outside Europe was not entirely possible.

The tension centring on the question of Europe's borders was made real by the lack of information about the region. Ancient sources, notably Ptolemy's geography and the writings of Herodotus, Strabo, Pliny, and others, provided some clues. There was also general knowledge of the once great Kyivan-Rus' Empire. But these were fragments from the past that had been swallowed up by the sea of tribes from the east, the threat of which had once even menaced the European heartland. Therefore, to make sense of the region, such that it might yet be reclaimed for Europe, new and more complete information was required. This would necessarily be obtained in the form of reports from travellers, which, although scarce and even harder to assess, became part of the narrative of Renaissance discovery. In the meantime, however, the classical sources would have to do.

Of all of the classical accounts, Ptolemy's *Geographia* would exert the most influence on early modern cartography. Reproduced and then supplemented by additional maps, numerous editions of the *Geographia* would be published in the fifteenth and sixteenth centuries, at least until the appearance of Abraham Ortelius' *Orbis Terrarum* made it obsolete. These new editions, especially those by Münster, Magini, and Gastaldi, enhanced the reputation of Ptolemy and of the ancient understanding of the world. In keeping with that understanding, which acknowledged the Black Sea as part of the Greek, and

later the Roman, world, the territory would be considered part of Europe, ending however at the Tanais, or Don, River. To underscore the point, features would be fabricated to delineate Europe from Asia. However, because the lands were associated in the European mind with barbarism, it was altogether appropriate, for instance in Girolamo Ruscelli's copy of Giacomo Gastladi's Ptolemaic map, to highlight the historical threat from the east by depicting a phalanx of barbarian tribes as assembling on Europe's frontier – Ukraine.

The work of Ptolemy, however, would not hold up under the discriminating and inquisitive mind of the Renaissance scholar Sebastian Münster, who sought out new information by instructing others on how to map their locales, while encouraging them to send descriptions to him for publication. The penultimate result, Münster's *Cosmographia*, which was reproduced in forty editions in six different languages, is one of the great achievements in European cartography. Chorographically detailed, the maps reflected a new approach to geography. Sources were identified and credited, while every effort was made to include amended maps in successive editions. The maps, printed in relief from woodblocks, were, of course, still crude representations with distortions and numerous inaccuracies: even the lettering from inset metal type would sometimes go astray in subsequent issues. Overall, however, the maps of Münster and his immediate successors – Abraham Ortelius and Gerard Mercator – marked an important departure in the acquisition, incorporation, and dissemination of geographical knowledge. Moreover, facilitated by innovative developments in publishing, notably the introduction of intaglio printing on durable copper plates, the new approach to cartography was soon imitated by others.

This is not to say that conventional ideas about the East disappeared. Rather, reinforced by reports from such travellers as Sigmund von Herberstein and Anthony Jenkinson, the East continued to be alien. An Italian edition of Ortelius' *Russiæ, Moscoviæ, Tartariæ* would, for example, include illustrations of some of the peculiar customs of the inhabitants that were based on descriptions found in von Herberstein's work. As for the political landscape, there continued to be much uncertainty. Lithuanian-Polish authority would be shown to extend to the Black Sea, for instance, in Matthew Quadt's *Polonia*, a 1594 rendition of Ortelius' earlier map of the region. But in practice the Pontic Steppe, although contested, was arguably under Tatar control. Muscovy, on the other hand, had not yet established political patrimony over the Rus' legacy. Consequently, because it was not yet part of an imagined landscape, a distinction would still be made between Muscovy and the ancient lands of Rus', as is evident in the title of Ortelius' map – *Russiæ, Moscoviæ, Tartariæ.*

M. Quadt, *Polonia* (1594)

A. Jenkinson/A. Ortelius, *Russiæ, Moscoviæ, Tartariæ* (1598)

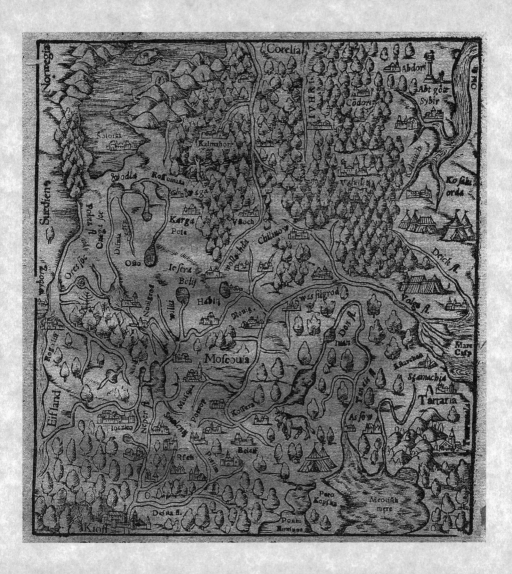

S. Münster, *Tartaria, Moscovia* (c.1565)

A. Ortelius, *Pontus Euxinus*, 1612 (detail)

According to the ancient Greek chronicler Strabo, the sea known as Pontus Euxinus was in Homer's time considered unnavigable because of the "wintery storms and the ferocity of the tribes that lived around it." It was not until the Ionian Greeks colonized the coast in the seventh century BC that the name of the sea changed from *Axenos* (inhospitable) to *Euxeinos* (friendly to strangers). To the extent that the Black Sea provided fish and the Scythian steppes grain, the region continued to lure the Greeks, who were impressed by its potential. Some eighteen centuries later, this was also true of the Genoese and Venetian merchants, who, tolerated by the ruling Mongol Golden Horde, established posts in the Crimea and on

A. Ortelius, *Pontus Euxinus* (1612)

G. Mercator/W. Blaeu, *Taurica Chersonesus* (1635)

G. Mercator/J. Hondius, *Taurica Chersonesus* (c. 1635)

N. Sanson, *De Zwarte Zee, eertyts Pontus Euxinus* (1683)

N. Witsen/R. and J. Ottens, *Pontus Euxinus of Niewe en Naaukeurige Paskaart van de Zwarte Zee* (c. 1697)

G. De L'Isle/ J. Covens and C. Mortier, *Seconde Partie de la Crimée, Le Mer Noire* (c. 1707) the banks of the Sea of Azov for purposes of trade in furs, caviar, and spices, but above all in slaves. All of this, however, would change in 1475, when in the fresh afterglow of the Ottoman seizure of Constantinople, the Turks, turning their sights on the Crimean Tatary, would chase the Venetians and Genoese out of the Black Sea basin, effectively making it a "Turkish lake." The Sea of Azov, the Black Sea, and the adjoining plains would become inaccessible as the faultlines of civilization were soon drawn between Christianity and Islam. The unfamiliar became "inhospitable" once again, conjuring up alien images that would forever affix the label of *Ukrania* to the region – Europe's borderland.

The period of Ottoman hegemony over the Black Sea and Pontic Steppe meant that cartographic information would be derived largely, but not exclusively, from preexisting sources or Turkish accounts. Moreover, since most sixteenth-century maps made by European cartographers were imitations of one another, they tended to repeat many of the same observations. In a great many of the maps, Italian place-names associated with trading posts – Moncastro, Bono Porto, San Giorgo, Paparoma, Pisan – recur again and again, as do oblique references to ancient Greek colonies – Olbia, Theodosia, Panticapaeum, Parthenium, and Symbolium – as in the case of Ortelius' *Pontus Euxinus*. Notwithstanding the repetition, there are certain peculiarities associated with each. For instance, in Ortelius' map, there can be found a passing reference to the Greek ruins on the Peninsula of Chersonesus and notations based on legends, conventions, and the accounts of the ancient

chroniclers Herodotus, Pliny, and Ovid. Ortelius' map, which is taken from a posthumous 1612 edition of his atlas *Theatrum Orbis Terrarum*, is also noteworthy for the chaotic interspersion of names of pre-Slav tribes (Antes, Iazyges, Roxolani, Gerrhus, Bastarnae) – a rudimentary attempt at linking historical time with geography.

In general, however, Ortelius' map, like Blaeu's copy of Mercator's *Taurica Chersonsesus* – an exquisite map that eschews the cumbersome block technique of engraved place-names in favour of Mercator's elegant ornamental style – provides only the most basic information on the Black Sea lowlands, attesting to the region's forbidden character. It was not until the late seventeenth century that data culled from Turkish sources allowed a relatively more complete description of the Black Sea to develop. For example, Reiner and Joshua Ottens' 1745 copy of Nicholas Witsen's map of 1697, sent originally by Peter I to Amsterdam to be engraved, is replete with Turkish names, as is Guillaume De L'Isle's map of the Black Sea basin, which appeared in his *Atlas de Géographie* of 1707 and was reproduced by the firm Covens & Mortier in 1733. Of the few Slavic toponyms found on the Witsen/Ottens map, there is mention of a *Dolina Zernaja* near the Dnipro estuary, a faint reference to grain production in the area, which served as the commercial mainstay in the relationship between the local Scythians and early Greek colonists. The term *Ucrana*, which also appears on the Witsen map and covers the steppes inhabited by the Nogay Tatars, is an assignation that identifies the territory more generally as a borderland rather than as a specific political designation. Turkish naval bases are identified on the De L'Isle map, pointing to the growing interest in the military capability of the Ottoman Empire.

It was shortly after an epitome of Ortelius' folio *Theatrum* was published in 1577 that new small geographies began to appear alongside the grand atlases. The maps produced in these pocket atlases were for the most part replicas of the folio-sized versions. They were often accompanied by the same text and duplicated the same features with the same attention to detail. Hondius' *Atlas Minor* of 1635, reproduced in numerous editions in all the major European languages, contained the map *Taurica Chersonesus*, which was based on Mercator's work. In keeping with market demand, pocket atlases in the seventeenth century sought to incorporate new geographic information. Inasmuch as this new information was blended with the old, a curious original resulted from the process, as was the case with the Black Sea map created by the great French cartographer Nicholas Sanson, which was reproduced in the posthumous Dutch edition of *Description de tout l'Univers* of 1683.

G. Mercator/J. Hondius, *Taurica Chersonesus* (c. 1635)

N. Sanson, *De Zwarte Zee, eertyts Pontus Euxinus* (1683)

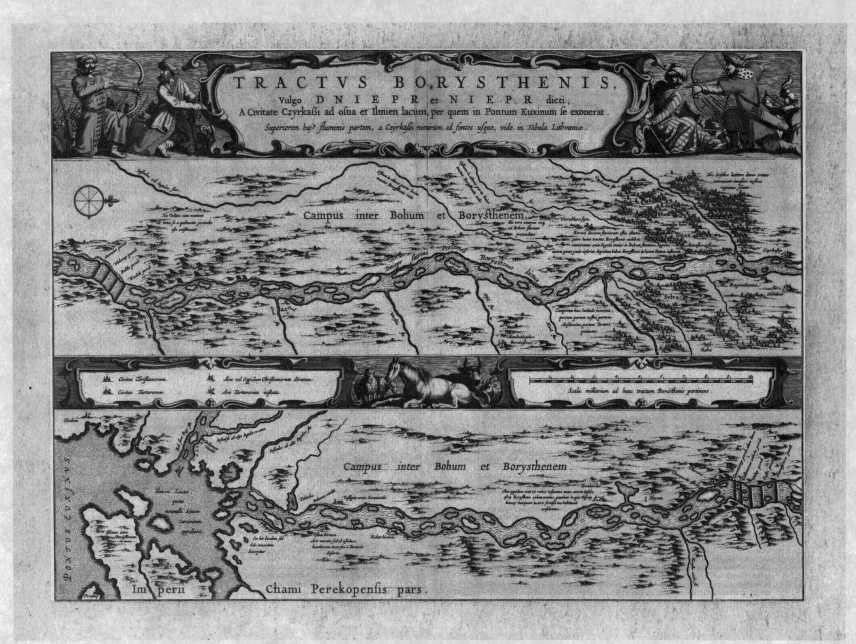

TRACTVS BORYSTHENIS,
Vulgo *D N I E P R* et *N I E P R* dicti,
A Civitate Czyrkaßi ad ostia et Ilmien lacum, per quem in Pontum Euxinum se exonerat.
Superiorem huj⁹ fluminis partem, a Czyrkaßi nimirum ad fontes usque, vide in Tabula Lithvaniæ.

Campus inter Bohum et Borysthenem

Campus inter Bohum et Borysthenem.

Im perii Chami Perekopensis pars.

W. Blaeu, *Tractus Borysthenis … a Civitate Czyrkasi ad ostia et Ilmien lacum* (1662)

T he southern steppes of Ukraine in the mid-sixteenth century presented both opportunity and danger. As an area contested by Poland and Ottoman Turkey, the Pontic Steppe served as a haven and refuge for those seeking fortune or relief from the burden of Poland's manorial system. But with frontier living there came trials and hazards: notably, a free but hard life punctuated by possible capture from Tatar slave-raiding parties from the south. Conditions and circumstances would eventually compel the resident frontiersmen to organize collectively for self-defence. In time, as their role changed, they would become known as Cossacks, from the Turkic word *qazaq* – a warrior freeman. In particular, buccaneering directed at Tatar trade

W. Blaeu, *Campus Inter Bohum* (c. 1635)

W. Blaeu, *Tractus Borysthenis ... a Civitate Czyrkasi ad ostia et Ilmien lacum* (1662)

W. Blaeu, *Tractus Borysthenis ... a Kiovia usque ad Bouzin* (1662)

W. Blaeu, *Tractus Borysthenis ... a Bouzin usque ad Chrotyca Ostrow* (1662)

W. Blaeu, *Tractus Borysthenis ... a Chortika Ostrow ad Urbem Oczakow* (1662)

W. Blaeu, *Campus Inter Bohum* (c. 1635)

Cherkasy on the Dnipro River earned a particular reputation as a centre of Cossack life, but for the more adventurous there was the *sich*. Situated in advance of and later relocated beyond the treacherous cataracts of the Dnipro (*za porohamy*), the *sich* became the military stronghold of the *nyzhni kozaky*, or the Zaporozhian Cossacks, as they were called. Attracting thousands to its ranks in the early seventeenth century, the Cossack movement, as an evolving autonomous military force, became an important factor in Polish domestic politics and in regional politics more generally.

In European circles the Cossacks were an unknown political quantity, but their notoriety as marauder-raiders grew as travellers, traders, diplomats, and others journeying to the east reported on their activities, customs, and habits. Published accounts would appear, perhaps the most important being the celebrated *Description d'Ukranie* of Guillaume Le Vasseur de Beauplan. A French military engineer attached to the army of the Polish crown as a captain of the artillery, he spent seventeen years in Ukraine (1630–47), during which he completed several remarkable maps of both Ukraine and the Dnipro River. The map of the Dnipro, produced as part of a military survey which he conducted in 1639, would appear in four consecutive folio sheets of two sections each in volume 2 of the 1662 edition of Blaeu's *Atlas Maior*. With great precision and attention to detail, the course of the river is outlined from Kyiv through Cherkasy to the Black Sea liman, as are settlements, roads, and ruins. Reference is also made to the Cossacks and their *sich* beyond the cataracts near the

caravans and commercial centres in the Islamic world, as well as payment for military services rendered for those registered with the Polish crown, became dominant aspects of Cossack activity. Two types of Cossacks emerged socially: those who would inhabit fortified towns along the frontier and those who preferred living outside political structures. The town of as a specific political designation. Turkish naval bases are identified on the De L'Isle map, pointing to the growing interest in the military capability of the Ottoman Empire.

It was shortly after an epitome of Ortelius' folio *Theatrum* was published in 1577 that new small geographies began to appear alongside the grand atlases. The maps produced in these pocket atlases were for the most part replicas of the folio-sized versions. They were often accompanied by the same text and duplicated the same features with the same attention to detail. Hondius' *Atlas Minor* of 1635, reproduced in numerous editions in all the major European languages, contained the map *Taurica Chersonesus*, which was based on Mercator's work. In keeping with market demand, pocket atlases in the seventeenth century sought to incorporate new geographic information. Inasmuch as this new information was blended with the old, a curious original resulted from the process, as was the case with the Black Sea map created by the great French cartographer Nicholas Sanson, which was reproduced in the posthumous Dutch edition of *Description de tout l'Univers* of 1683.

G. Mercator/J. Hondius, *Taurica Chersonesus* (c. 1635)

N. Sanson, *De Zwarte Zee, eertyts Pontus Euxinus* (1683)

W. Blaeu, *Tractus Borysthenis … a Civitate Czyrkasi ad ostia et Ilmien lacum* (1662)

T he southern steppes of Ukraine in the mid-sixteenth century presented both opportunity and danger. As an area contested by Poland and Ottoman Turkey, the Pontic Steppe served as a haven and refuge for those seeking fortune or relief from the burden of Poland's manorial system. But with frontier living there came trials and hazards: notably, a free but hard life punctuated by possible capture from Tatar slave-raiding parties from the south. Conditions and circumstances would eventually compel the resident frontiersmen to organize collectively for self-defence. In time, as their role changed, they would become known as Cossacks, from the Turkic word *qazaq* – a warrior freeman. In particular, buccaneering directed at Tatar trade

W. Blaeu, *Campus Inter Bohum* (c. 1635)

W. Blaeu, *Tractus Borysthenis ... a Civitate Czyrkasi ad ostia et Ilmien lacum* (1662)

W. Blaeu, *Tractus Borysthenis ... a Kiovia usque ad Bouzin* (1662)

W. Blaeu, *Tractus Borysthenis ... a Bouzin usque ad Chrotyca Ostrow* (1662)

W. Blaeu, *Tractus Borysthenis ... a Chortika Ostrow ad Urbem Oczakow* (1662)

W. Blaeu, *Campus Inter Bohum* (c. 1635)

Cherkasy on the Dnipro River earned a particular reputation as a centre of Cossack life, but for the more adventurous there was the *sich*. Situated in advance of and later relocated beyond the treacherous cataracts of the Dnipro (*za porohamy*), the *sich* became the military stronghold of the *nyzhni kozaky*, or the Zaporozhian Cossacks, as they were called. Attracting thousands to its ranks in the early seventeenth century, the Cossack movement, as an evolving autonomous military force, became an important factor in Polish domestic politics and in regional politics more generally.

In European circles the Cossacks were an unknown political quantity, but their notoriety as marauder-raiders grew as travellers, traders, diplomats, and others journeying to the east reported on their activities, customs, and habits. Published accounts would appear, perhaps the most important being the celebrated *Description d'Ukranie* of Guillaume Le Vasseur de Beauplan. A French military engineer attached to the army of the Polish crown as a captain of the artillery, he spent seventeen years in Ukraine (1630–47), during which he completed several remarkable maps of both Ukraine and the Dnipro River. The map of the Dnipro, produced as part of a military survey which he conducted in 1639, would appear in four consecutive folio sheets of two sections each in volume 2 of the 1662 edition of Blaeu's *Atlas Maior*. With great precision and attention to detail, the course of the river is outlined from Kyiv through Cherkasy to the Black Sea liman, as are settlements, roads, and ruins. Reference is also made to the Cossacks and their *sich* beyond the cataracts near the

caravans and commercial centres in the Islamic world, as well as payment for military services rendered for those registered with the Polish crown, became dominant aspects of Cossack activity. Two types of Cossacks emerged socially: those who would inhabit fortified towns along the frontier and those who preferred living outside political structures. The town of river island of Tomakivka. The published maps are accompanied by a Latin text, verso, taken from his *Description* which offers an account of the Cossacks, while likenesses of Cossack figures feature prominently in the richly decorated and finely crafted cartouches, for which the Dutch firm of Blaeu was renowned.

The Beauplan maps that appeared in Blaeu's *Atlas Maior* were not the first maps of the Dnipro River to be published. Rather, an earlier depiction of the Dnipro created by the Polish chronicler and painter T. Makowsky, commissioned by the Lithuanian Prince Janusz Radziwill, and engraved by H. Gerritz as an inset in a larger compilation on the Polish-Lithuanian Commonwealth appeared in Blaeu's 1631 version of the earlier Mercator-Hondius *Atlas.* The inset, published as a separate map in 1635, contains annotations on the Cossacks, the Cossack Hetman Dmytro Vyshnevets'kyi, and the *sich*, as well as on the cataracts. Christian Cossack and Muslim Tatar settlements are identified along its course. The Makowsky map generated interest in the region, especially as news of the exploits of the Cossacks became more widely known. In general, however, the southern reaches of the Dnipro and Black Sea steppes were alien territory, and those who ventured there courted disaster. Consequently, cartographic information would remain scarce. The Muscovite tsar Peter I, who possessed neither a map of the Dnipro nor data on the cataracts, would charge Hetman Ivan Mazepa in 1696 with preparing a map of the river. That map was apparently drawn, but the document has not survived.

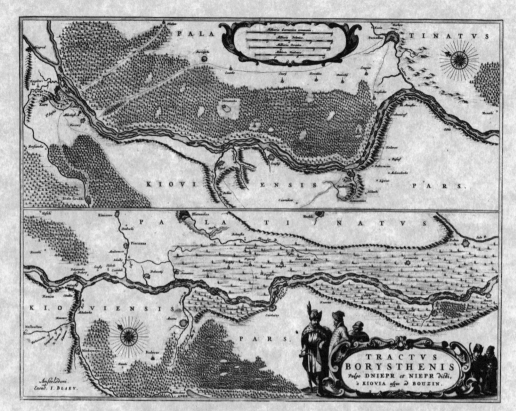

W. Blaeu, *Tractus Borysthenis … a Kiovia usque ad Bouzin* (1662)

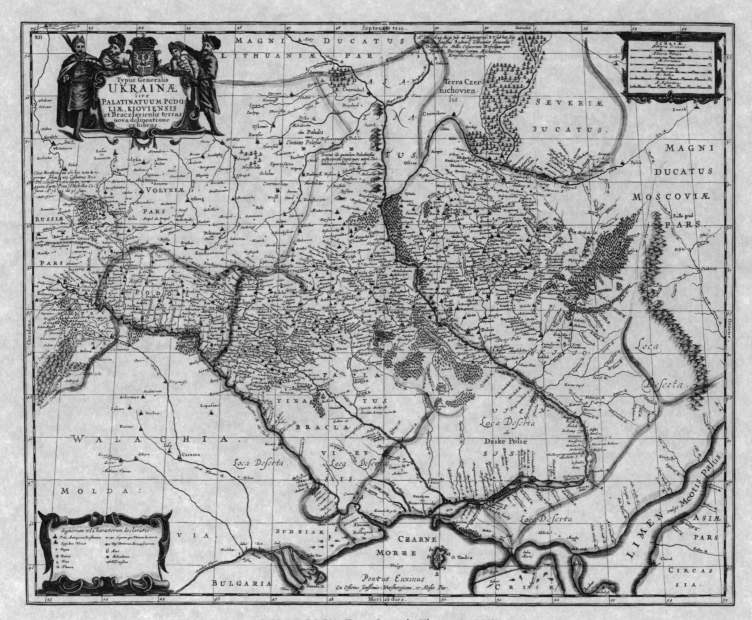

J. Jansson/M. Pitt, *Typus Generalis Ukrainæ* (c. 1660)

T he Cossacks who were seeking to
secure greater privileges from the Polish crown and who were in com-
petition with Polish nobility and landed gentry, proved to be an unpre-
dictable force. Rebellions in the early half of the seventeenth century
were only the harbinger of a much larger social and political revolu-
tion, which, after a series of successive victories over the Polish crown
army in 1648–49, resulted in the formation of a Cossack state. The
Cossack state, centred on the Army of the Zaporozhia or Zaporozhian
Host, as it was called, came into its own politically after the Treaty of
Zboriv (1649). Quasi-democratic yet hierarchical, it was an anomaly in
European politics, inasmuch as it was organized along regional regimental

J. Jansson/M. Pitt, *Typus Generalis Ukrainæ* (c. 1660)

J. Homman, *Ukrania quæ et Terra Cosaccorum* (1716)

J. Homman/C. Weigel, *Ukrania seu Cosacorum* (c. 1720)

M. Seutter/T. Lotter, *Amplissima Ukraniæ Regio* (c. 1720)

lines and administered through a military command structure. Encompassing the central lands of Ukraine on both sides of the Dnipro River, from Chernihiv/Chornobyl in the north to the *sich* in the south and from Podolia in the west to the Mokarsky trade route in the east, the Cossack state would be identified in period maps with the term Ukraine, as is the case in Matthäus Seutter's map *Amplissima Ukraniæ Regio* of 1720.

In the face of external threats, its diffused governance proved to be the undoing of the short-lived Cossack state (1649–57). Moreover, failed diplomacy would plunge the Cossack lands into a state of continuous war lasting some three decades. Referred to as the Period of Ruin in Ukrainian historiography, the territory was divided along the Dnipro between Poland (Right Bank Ukraine) and Muscovy (Left Bank Ukraine), while the former Polish palatinates of Podolia and Bratslav and a large stretch of territory south of Kyiv would come under the control of Ottoman Turkey between 1672 and 1699. Although traditional Cossack rights and liberties continued to be recognized by the Muscovite tsars in Left Bank Ukraine, the Ukrainian lands under Muscovy's influence – the Hetmanate and Zaporozhia – became an important factor in Muscovy's expansionist efforts against the Turkish sultan, especially under Peter I. The perceived threat to the collective interests of the Cossacks would eventually compel the Cossack leader Hetman Ivan Mazepa to side with Sweden's Charles XII in the Great Northern War (1700–21). In one of those decisive battles that would change the course of world history, a combined Swedish-Cossack force was defeated at the battle of Poltava in 1709. That defeat would have serious consequences for Cossack autonomy, since soon thereafter the Hetmanate and Zaporozhia became directly integrated into the social, political, and economic structure of the Russian Empire. As for Russia, at the end of hostilities with Sweden in 1721 it emerged in its own right as a contender for political power in European affairs.

Despite the changing political situation that made for much uncertainty, publishers of maps attempted to keep abreast of developments to the east. The Cossack state, for instance, was part of the repertoire of the major mapmakers and publishers in Europe. There were, in particular, several outstanding maps of the Cossack state, notably those of J.B. Homman, Matthäus Seutter, and J. Jansson. Typically, they outlined the territorial extent of Cossack authority and the location of the Cossack *sich*. In the region of the southern steppes the lands are often described as *Dzike Pole* or *Campi Deserti et Inhabitati*, terms that refer to the sparsely populated nature of the frontier with the Crimean Khanate. To the extent that the maps were produced after the demise of the Cossack state, there are also occasional references to recent events. *Typus Generalis Ukrainæ*, a map that first appeared in the Dutch edition (1657–59) of Jan Jansson's *Novus Atlas* and that was later reproduced by his heirs (it was taken originally from the work of the great cartographer Beauplan), contains, for instance, several such references, including a notation on the Polish victory over Cossack forces at the battle of Berestechko (1651), a turning point in the fortunes of the Cossack state. But perhaps most striking is the representation in the cartouche that adorns Homman's map *Ukrania quæ et Terra Cosaccorum*, a transparent reference to the figures of Mazepa, Charles XII, and Peter I, whose fates were determined at the battle of Poltava.

Atlases and maps enjoyed great popularity in the early eighteenth century among a clientele eager for more information. To augment the presentation of the maps, Europe's finest illustrators were employed by the leading firms to create title pieces that would satisfy the aesthetic sensibility of a buying public while also conveying thematically, as was done in Christoph Weigel's *Ukrania seu Cosacorum*, the essence of the map; in this case, a vignette portraying a Cossack encampment. Equally charming is the cartouche in Seutter's *Amplissima Ukraniæ Regio*, a fanciful allegorical allusion to Ukraine's natural abundance.

J.B. Homman, *Ukrania quæ et Terra Cosaccorum* (1716)

UKRANIA seu COSACORI
Regio Walachia item Moldav
et Tartaria minor
exc: Christ: Weigelio Norib:

30

J. Homman/C. Weigel, *Ukrania seu Cosacorum*, c. 1720 (detail)

31

J. N. Bellin, *Plan d'Azak où Azof* (1764)

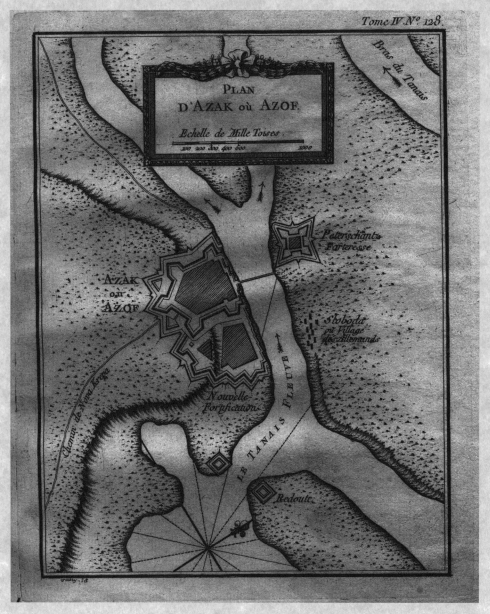

The Ottoman Empire was vitally important in Muscovy's power bid to become a European player. But if the Porte was central to Muscovy's plans, then the Turkish fortress at Azak or Azov – formerly the Venetian fortress of Tana, located on the delta of the mighty Don River – was pivotal. Control of the fort meant access to the Sea of Azov and, potentially, to the Black Sea beyond. The young Tsar Peter I, bent on conquest, would attack the fort in 1695. Initial failure was followed by success in 1696, when a flotilla of ships, freshly constructed at Voronezh, sailed down the Don River to the sea and helped cut Turkish supply lines in the renewed effort to seize the fortified town. The victory over the Porte would impress the Europeans.

C. Rugell/M. Seutter, *Nova Mappa Geographica Mari Assoviensis vel de Zabache et Paludis Mæotidis* (1699)

C. Cruys/ R. Ottens, *Nieuwe zeer Accurate, en Nauukeurige Caart van de Rivier den Don of Tanais* (1699)

J. N. Bellin, *Carte des Embouchures du Tanais* (1764)

J. N. Bellin, *Plan d'Azak où Azof* (1764)

But in gaining a southern outlet, the idea of Muscovy as strictly a northern land was also forever altered. The strategic importance of the Azov fortress – lost to the Turks in 1713 and regained in 1739 – was underscored by the continuing appearance, well into the latter half of the eighteenth century, of maps that described the approaches to and configuration of the citadel. Particularly fine examples of such maps were created by the eminent French hydrographer Jacques Nicolas Bellin for his multivolume *Petit Atlas Maritime,* published in 1764.

The significance of mapping the lower Don region would greatly increase after Muscovy's victory over the Porte. If there was to be a political claim to the lands, then there had to be an understanding of the nature of the claim. But this meant information. It was immediately decided that a survey of the Don River had to be undertaken. Little time was wasted, and material was collected in 1697. However, it was not until 1699 that a more comprehensive survey was conducted by the vice admiral of the newly created Russian Navy, the Dutchman Cornelius Cruys, as part of an expedition that would navigate down the Don River, penetrate the Straits of Kerch, and eventually make its way on to Istanbul.

The Cruys expedition provided a rare opportunity for maps to be drawn not only of the Don but also of the Sea of Azov, the Black Sea, the Bosporus, and some relief portions of the Black Sea coast. Specialists accompanying the mission prepared individual maps. The Swedish engineer Christian Rugell, for instance, was responsible for drawing a manuscript map of the Sea of Azov, which would appear a few years later in Nicholas Visscher's *Atlas Minor* and subsequently reproduced in 1720 by the firm of Matthäus Seutter. As for the maps of the Don River that were prepared by Cruys personally, these would be published as part of a special atlas of the river prepared in Amsterdam by the Dutch publisher Hendrick Doncker in 1705. The maps in manuscript form were sent by Cruys to be engraved and printed in the Netherlands, because production facilities did not yet exist in Muscovy. This would soon change, however, because of the political value associated with map production. The Don River manuscript maps were in fact the last to be produced abroad.

Among the maps included in the Don River atlas was a general two-sheet map depicting the course of the river. It included an inset of the harbour at Azov and the seaside depot at Taganrog. A version of the map containing new information on the river's source and the Don-Volga canal would appear in Reiner Ottens' *Atlas Maior* (c. 1729). An interesting feature of the map is the delineated frontier between the administrative area of Belgorod and the lands inhabited by Ukrainian Cossacks (*Ocrainese Cosacken*). This territory, part of an autonomous region known as Sloboda Ukraine, provided refuge in the latter half of the seventeenth century for those Cossacks who moved eastward in response to the decades of conflict in central Ukraine. The Cruys map also shows elevations, dates of night anchorages, and geographical points of interest along the course of the river. In keeping with the scientific-technical nature of the Cruys mission, the practice of including unexplored tributaries was discontinued, highlighting the evolution in cartography, according to which mapping, once the special preserve of the painter-miniaturist, was now in the hands of civil-military engineers and navigators.

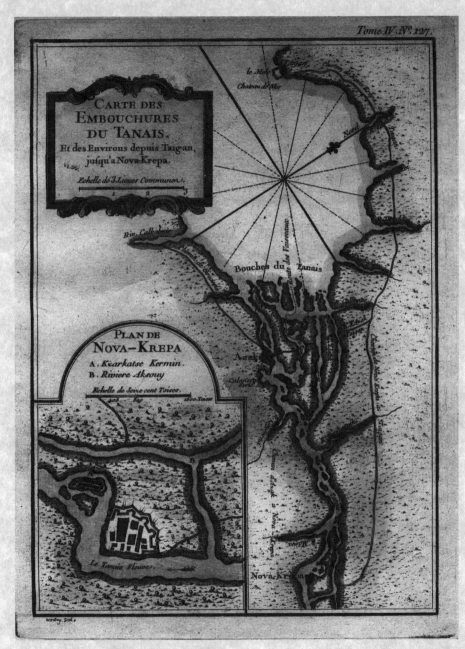

J. N. Bellin, *Carte des Embouchures du Tanais* (1764)

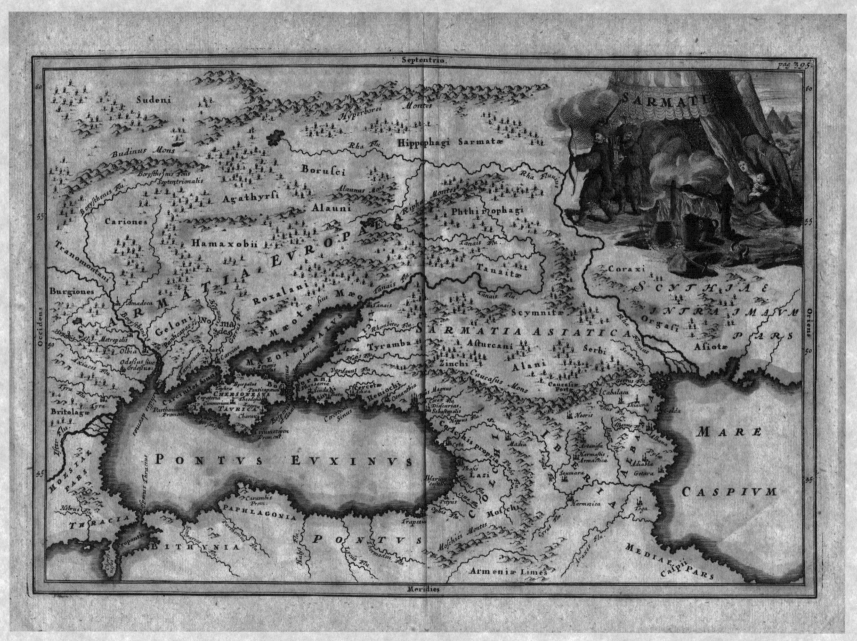

Septentrio.

pag 305.

SARMATIA

Sudeni

Hyperborei   Montes

Rha Flu.   Hippophagi Sarmatæ

Rha fluuius

Budinus Mons

Borussci

Borysthenis Fons
Septentrionalis

Alaunus   Montes

Agathyrsi

Alauni

Coraxi

SCYTHIÆ

Cariones

Phthirophagi

Hamaxobii

SARMATIA EVROPAEA

Ripha

Tanais Flu.

Tanaitæ

INTRA IMAVM

Orgasi

PARS

Asiotæ

Tranomontani

Roxalani   sive Mæo

Tanais Flu.

Tanais Flu.

Scymnitæ

Burgiones

Geloni

Noss   ma
des

Rhembetes Fla.

SARMATIA ASIATICA

Asturcani

Serbi

SARMATIA

MEOTIS PALVS

Tanais

Zinchi

Alani

Caucasus Mons

Caucasiæ
Portæ

Metropolis

Olbia

Odessus siue
Ordessus

CHERSONESVS

TAVRICA

Corani

Cercetæ

Heniochi

Discurias
Sebaltopolis

Noeris

Cabalaca

MARE

Britolagæ

Theodosia

Charax

Triumetopon
Prom. cont.

Cercetæ Sinus

COLCHIS

IBERIA

CASPIVM

MOESIAE

PARS

PONTVS EVXINVS

propria

Phasis

Lazi

Soumara

Gotara

THRACIA

Carambis
Prom.

PAPHLAGONIA

Moschi

Harmozica

MEDIAE

CASPII PARS

BITHYNIA

PONTVS

Moschici Montes

Trapezus

Armeniæ Limes

Meridies.

Occidens   Oriens

60

55

50

45

40

C. Cellarius, *Sarmatia* (1731)

 is placed above; the decorative cartouche with the Roman numeral VI.

T he question of where Europe's natural borders were located was historically a difficult one. Until the early eighteenth century, there was no clear answer and indeed much speculation. Offering some guidance in the matter, Classical accounts identified civilization's frontier to be at the Tanais, or Don, River, in that it marked the furthest extent of Greek colonization. But European civilization had been displaced, certainly in the area of the Black Sea, by the Tatar-Mongol horde from the east. Hence the problem. It was of course psychologically possible to shift the frontier westward, and in fact there was much to recommend the logic favouring a culturally homogenous Europe in the West. But then how were the embattled

J. Jansson, *Tab. II. Asiæ. Sarmatiam Asiaticam repræsentans* (c. 1680)

A. Mallet, *Sarmatie Europeenne* (1683)

C. Cellarius, *Sarmatia* (1731)

Poles and Lithuanians, who were outwardly European, to be explained? The ancient view that the land to the immediate east – Sarmatia – was part of Europe would be admitted, but in so doing *Ukrania* – the borderland – would necessarily be its frontier.

This Classical view, which informed the early modern geography of Europe, would endure throughout much of the seventeenth century. Historical maps, produced for interest sake and circulating at the time, reinforced the perspective. An example was Jan Jansson's reissue in his *Accuratissima orbis Antiqui Delineatio* of an early Ptolemaic map that made the distinction between Europe and Asia along the Tanais/Don River. Other atlases of the period containing both contemporary and historical maps, such as Alain Mallet's popular and informative miniature atlas *Description de l'Univers* (1683), would also repeat the Classical notion that European Sarmatia was distinct and that its frontiers coincided with the Don. However, this perspective would gradually change as a result of the extraordinary developments occurring in Muscovy in the late seventeenth and early eighteenth century.

Territorial expansion and the emergence of an administrative state, as well as a series of decisive military victories over nearby adversaries, altered the fortunes of Muscovy and in the process the traditional perspective on frontiers. No longer Muscovy but the Russian Empire, its place in Europe was secure by the early- to mid-seventeenth century, especially since influential Europeans – Voltaire, Jaucourt, and others – would acknowledge the change in Russia and its growing role in European affairs. Accordingly, a num-ber of historical maps, such as Christoph Cellarius' *Sarmatia*, with its delightful cartouche, which was published in a posthumous 1731 edition of his atlas *Nucleus geographæ antiquæ et novæ* (1686), would show the frontier of Europe further to the east, and *Sarmatia Asiatica* pushed back to the Caucasus. Critically, this new paradigm would influence the manner in which Russia would subsequently be depicted in maps: that is to say as having both a European and an Asian dimension, but with Europe's frontiers now situated at the Volga.

Despite the conceptual shift in the frontier landscape, the status of Ukraine as a borderland would not change. A North-South divide replaced the East-West axis, a consequence of the cultural and political fault that existed between Christianity and Islam and that cut directly across the Black Sea steppes.

A. Mallet, *Sarmatie Europeenne* (1683)

J. G. Schreiber, *Die Europæische oder Kleine Tartarey nebst den Angraentzenden Lændern* (1749)

VII

T he expansionist nature of the Russian Empire would inevitably lead to another round of hostilities with the Porte. The territorial concessions negotiated as part of the Treaty of Prut (1711), especially the loss of the fortress at Azov, did not agree with the imperial court at St Petersburg. After a false start in 1735, in a major offensive that would eventually lead them to the Crimea, a Russian army crossed the Izium Line – a fortified line of defensive positions along the Orel and Berestowa Rivers – while to the east the stronghold at Azov was besieged. The war, a bloody affair that ravaged the countryside, ended inconclusively four years later. The main objective, control over the fortress at Azov, was achieved. But it

G. De L'Isle/R. and J. Ottens, *Nouvelle Carte de La Petite Tartariæ et La Mer Noire* (c.1739)

P. Schenk/H. de Leth, *Carte de la Petite Tartarie* (c. 1739)

G. M. Seutter, *Nova et accurata Turcicarum et Tartaricarum Provinciarum* (c. 1744)

J. G. Schreiber, *Die Europæische oder Kleine Tartarey nebst den Angraentzenden Lændern* (1749) was a hollow victory. Under the terms of the peace, the citadel was dismantled, the naval depot at Taganrog was abandoned, Russian vessels excluded from the Black Sea, and trade was to be conducted only through intermediary Turkish vessels. This unsatisfactory arrangement would necessarily result in yet another war some thirty years later.

The Russo-Turkish war of 1735–39 sparked European interest in the events to the east and in turn created a demand for maps of the region. Assorted maps were produced both during and after the conflict. The cartographic work of Guillaume De L'Isle served as the foundation for many of these maps, including Ottens' copy entitled *Nouvelle Carte de La Petite Tartariæ et La Mer Noire*. An outstanding geographer, De L'Isle assumed a critical approach to his predecessors, preferring instead to base his work on meticulous scientific observations while using only corroborated information. In the process he would produce a body of work that would earn him a reputation deserving the title Premier Géographe du Roi. *Nouvelle Carte de la Petite Tartariæ* contains a number of interesting features, including the Izium, or "Ukrainian," Line as it was called, as well as a Cossack encampment south of Kizi-Kirmen (Beryslav) at the juncture of the Inhulets and Dnipro Rivers. Ottoman naval bays located on the Anatolian coast and Crimea are also indicated, as are the Crimean residences of the Khan and the Grand Vizier.

Other maps that would detail the conflict included those produced by the firm of Matthäus Seutter. His *Atlas Minor* of 1744 contained the map *Nova et accurata Turcicarum et Tartaricarum*

Provinciarum which is an exact copy of an earlier but larger folio map produced by the firm titled *Theatrum Belli Russorum Victoriis*. A curious feature of this miniaturized map is the reference to the *novaja setsch* (*nova sich*) south of the Inhulets River near Oleshky, on Tatar territory. Several thousand Zaporozhian Cossacks retreated to this area after the defeat at Poltava in 1709 and built a *sich*. They remained in exile there under the protection of the Crimean Khan, until an amnesty in 1734 allowed them to return near the site of the old Zaporozhian *sich* (*Saporoger Setsh*) situated further to the north, along the curvature of the Dnipro River.

Seutter's *Atlas Minor* was but one of a great many quarto-sized atlases produced at the time. Extremely popular, they were scaled to meet the budget of a wider clientele. What they would lack in quality, they would more than compensate for in terms of information, as is the case with Johan Schreiber's *Die Europæische oder Kleine Tartarey*, a map published in his *Atlas Selectus* of 1740 (reissued 1749). As for the specialists, there were unique maps produced for such discriminating buyers. An unusual item, for example, is Peter Schenk's articulated map *Carte de la Petite Tartarie*, which outlines the Russian campaign in the steppes of Little Tatary, or, more commonly, the Crimean Khanate. It describes the quartering of the Russian army, the anchorages of the Azov flotilla, and defensive trenches at Perekop and the Dnipro estuary.

G. M. Seutter, *Nova et accurata Turcicarum et Tartaricarum Provinciarum* (c. 1744)

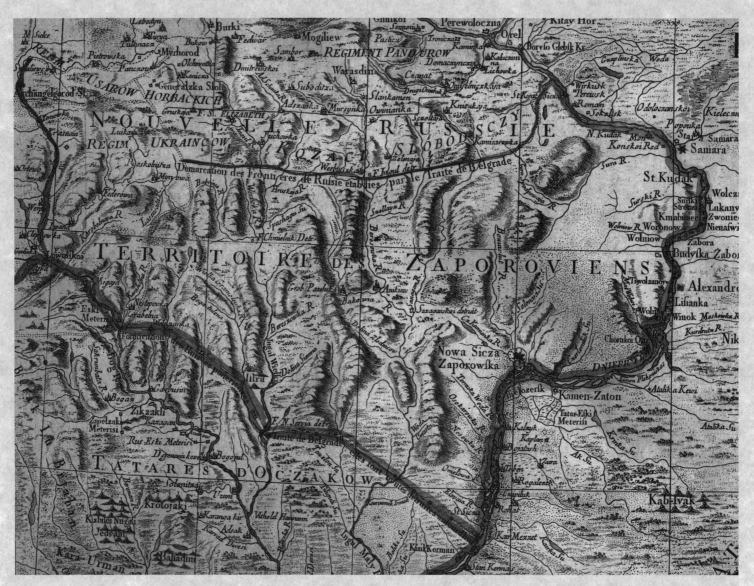

G. Rizzi-Zannoni, *La Crimée, La Nouvelle Russie, les Tartares Nugay*, 1774 (detail)

F rom Russia's perspective, the Russo-Turkish war of 1735–39 was an unmitigated disaster. The conflict resulted in huge losses: treasure was spent, casualties were high, and the Zaporozhian lands under Russian authority were devastated, while very little in the way of political gain was achieved. This setback, however, did not quell Russia's imperial ambitions. Russia became increasingly involved in Poland's domestic affairs, and at tremendous expense to the state treasury it continued to position itself against the Porte by colonizing the northern frontier of Zaporozhia on Right Bank Ukraine. The territory, designated as New Serbia (*Nouvelle Servie*), received an array of colonists from the Balkans – Serbs, Croats,

G. Robert de Vaugondy/F. Santini, *Carte des Envrions de la Mer Noire* (c.1769)

G. Rizzi-Zannoni, *La Crimée, La Nouvelle Russie, les Tartares Nugay* (1774)

T. Lotter, *Carte de Gouvernment de Tauride* (c. 1778)

Romanians, Bulgarians, and Greeks. All these developments alarmed Ottoman Turkey, but it was Russian incursions into Turkish territory in pursuit of Polish insurgents who were part of the ill-fated anti-Russian Confederacy of Bar that provided the actual pretext for war, which began in earnest in 1769.

Although the belligerents were evenly matched, the superior Russian navy, much improved in the intervening years, was a decisive factor. The war would conclude with the Treaty of Küçük-Kainarji (1774), yielding considerable dividends for Russia: the fort at Kinburn was ceded, as was the steppe between the Boh and Dnipro Rivers, although the important stronghold of Ochakiv at the mouth of the Dnipro River remained in the possession of the Porte. Additionally, Russian vessels had unrestricted access to the Black Sea, a point underscored by Russia retaining control over the sentinel fortresses at Kerch and Ienikale, which guarded the straits between the Black and Azov Seas. But perhaps most importantly, the Ottoman Empire was forced to relinquish its authority over land and fortresses in Crimea, in effect granting the Crimean Khanate independence in civil and political matters. Russia's military and political success over its southern adversary greatly increased Russian influence and control over the Pontic Steppe, which would have consequences for the still-autonomous Zaporozhian Cossacks, allies of Russia in its conflict with the Porte. Viewed as an impediment to future colonization, the Cossack *sich* – reestablished in 1734 near the site of the old *sich* – was razed under imperial order in 1775 by victorious Russian troops returning after their campaign in the Crimea to the south. The Cossacks were dispersed, and the Zaporozhian lands, formally annexed in 1775, were incorporated into the administrative territory known as New Russia.

The Russo-Turkish war of 1769–74 coincided with an exceptional period in cartography, which is reflected in the quality of the maps appearing on the Black Sea region. Systematic surveys and the wider use of astronomical observations for measurement made it possible to record with exacting precision an area that had not easily revealed itself. Moreover, master cartographers who were producing extraordinary maps at the time, in particular Gilles Robert de Vaugondy and Giovanni Rizzi-Zannoni, were carefully working with this information. The handsomely illustrated and finely engraved *Carte des Envrions de la Mer Noire,* for example, demonstrates Vaugondy's exemplary commitment to accuracy and detail. Originally published in 1769, the map provides information on *Nouvelle Servie*, an area that, according to Vaugondy, included fifty villages in 1754. The Russian-Turkish frontier is also identified as being garrisoned, and the defences are shown as consisting of three forts and twelve redoubts, unusual information for the day. More impressive, however, is Rizzi-Zannoni's map of the Crimea and the Pontic Steppe – *La Crimée, La Nouvelle Russie, les Tartares Nugay* – taken from the exquisite six-sheet compilation *Carte de la Partie Septerionale de L'Empire Otoman*, which shows in remarkable detail the area of the former New Serbia. Renamed New Russia in 1764, the map describes the administrative military organization of the territory, identifying in particular the location of frontier regiments – *Regiment Usarow Horbackich, Regiment Pandurow, Regiment Ukraincow* – as well as Cossacks recruited from the Sloboda Ukraine to the east. Finally, negotiated under the Treaty of Belgrade (1739), the limits of the Russo-Turkish frontier are shown, as is the territory of the neutral Zaporozhian Cossacks and their *sich* (*Nova Sicza Zaporowska*).

Russia's victory over the Porte forced the issue of Crimean sovereignty. Under Ottoman suzerainty since the fifteenth century, the independence of the Crimean Khanate was part of the peace agreement of 1774. Accordingly, maps of the Black Sea littoral that appeared after the conflict, including Tobias Lotter's *Carte de Gouvernment de Tauride* (c. 1778), would outline the borders of the independent Crimean state. But, as with the Lotter map, they would also, rather inauspiciously, begin to incorporate the changes occurring in the local toponymy of the newly acquired territories: Russian toponyms quickly replaced Tatar and Ukrainian place-names. Shortly after Russia's annexation of Crimea in 1783, the process of changing toponymy was accelerated, resulting by the end of the eighteenth century in the near disappearance from the cartographic record of most of the historical Tatar place-names associated with the Crimean peninsula and the Black Sea coast.

G. Robert de Vaugondy/F. Santini, *Carte des Envrions de la Mer Noire*, c.1769 (detail)

J. N. Bellin, *Carte de la Crimée* (1764)

M aterials on the Black Sea in the early eighteenth century were scarce, which is attested to by the fact that Nicholas Witsen's map of 1697, *Pontus Euxinus*, although wholly unsuitable for navigation, was included in L. Renard's special navigation atlas published in 1739. The difficulties associated with obtaining authoritative information on this body of water stemmed from the fact that it was closed, since the Porte, which was in control of the pivotal Bosporous and Kerch Straits, was in a position to deny access to foreign vessels. There were, of course, several important Black Sea maps published in the first half of the eighteenth century that provided a profile of the basin and information on coastal settlements; for instance,

J. N. Bellin, *Carte de la Crimée* (1764)

J. N. Bellin, *Carte de la Mer Noire* (1764)

J. N. Bellin, *Carte Réduite de la Mer Noire* (1772)

A. Kinsbergen, *Carte de la Mer d'Azof et d'une Partie de la Mer Noire* (1774)

J. Roux, *Rade de Kaffa ... Golfe d'Azof ... Detroit de Kertch* (1779)

De L'Isle's maps, which relied on Turkish sources. But despite these best efforts, the maps were largely impressionistic and far from accurate, the basin in most cases being excessively drawn out at the parallel, because of a lack of astronomically determined coastal points. In effect, the Black Sea was an enigma. Even the shape of the Crimean peninsula was open to speculation: J. Bellin's two maps of the Crimea and the Black Sea, for example, although published in separate volumes of his *Petit Atlas Maritime* of 1764, would curiously show the Crimea as being both round and trapezoid in shape. All of this, however, would change with the Russo-Turkish war of 1769–74.

The start of the conflict saw the creation of the Don/Azov fleet, consisting of nine frigates and an assortment of smaller vessels; instructions were also given to commence shipbuilding for a proposed Danube fleet, a project successfully undertaken in 1771. The Azov and Danube fleets, as well as Russian ships in the Aegean proved to be an important factor in Russia's victory over the Porte. Significantly, throughout the conflict, while plying the waters of the Black and Azov Seas, Russian naval commanders began collecting information for nautical charts: surveying the coast, taking soundings, identifying sandbars, and describing landmarks and harbours. The Dutchman A. Kinsbergen, captain second rank and commander of the Second Squadron of the Azov fleet made the most significant contribution in this regard. After defeating the Turkish fleet in a major naval engagement off Crimea's Cape Chersonesus in 1773 – a victory that allowed the Russian navy greater freedom – Kinsbergen devoted his attention to charting the waters and surveying the coast. The result was his map *Carte de la Mer d'Azof* (1774) and an additional four-sheet map of the Crimea, both widely acclaimed. He was also the author of an even larger map of the Sea of Azov, Crimea, and the northern Black Sea littoral, with inset plans of the Straits of Kerch, Cape Chersonesus, and the 'Golfa de Balaclava.' These materials appear to have been used by Joseph Roux for several maps in his octavio-sized atlas *Recueil des principaux plans des ports et rades de la Mer Mediteranée*, originally published in 1779. The Roux maps, which were finely engraved and exceptionally detailed, would provide vital information on passages, anchorages, and, more generally, profiles of the Crimean and Azov coastline.

The Russian naval presence in the Black Sea during the conflict with Ottoman Turkey would necessarily attract the attention of the other European powers who were concerned with imperial Russia's growing military capabilities. French officials commissioned Jacques Bellin, head of the newly created French Hydrographic Service, to produce a map of the Black Sea basin for the French Admiralty. Bellin's *Carte Réduite de la Mer Noire*, published in 1772 at the height of the conflict, was an improvement over existing European maps, but the coastal profile continued to be superficially described. Nevertheless, since Russian nautical charts of the Black Sea would not appear in circulation until several decades later, Bellin's map, which could be purchased at the time for *cinquante sous*, was used extensively by foreign navigators.

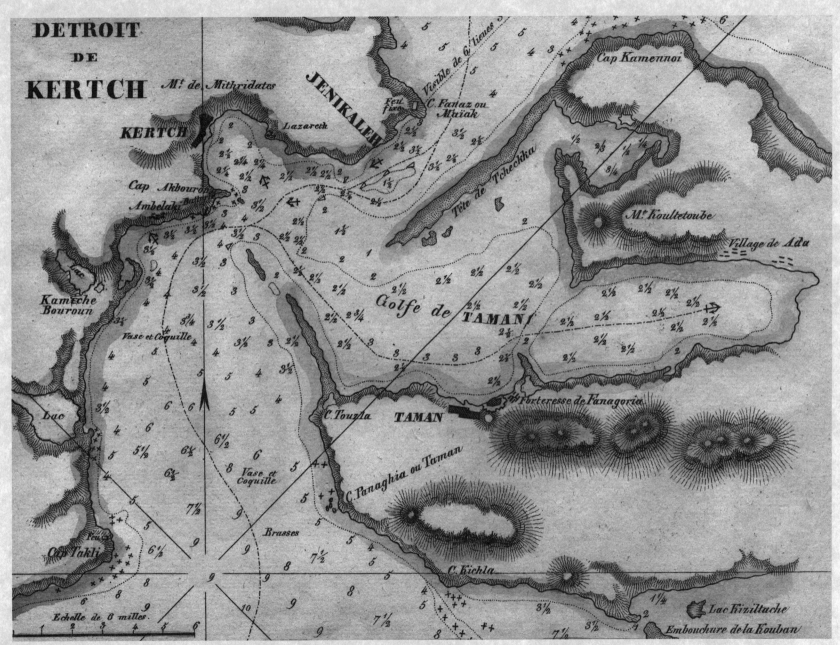

J. Roux, Detroit de Kertch (1779)

J. von Reilly, *Die Ostchakowische Tartarey oder Westliches Nogaj auch Jedisan* (1789)

Imperial Russia's victory over the Porte in a series of late-eighteenth-century wars would severely diminish the influence of Turkey in Europe, and in Ukraine in particular. As part of the Peace Treaty of Küçük-Kainarji, which concluded the war of 1769–74, the independence of the Crimean Khanate – a long-standing protectorate of Ottoman Turkey – was negotiated between the two protagonists, while the territory between the Dnipro and Boh Rivers, with the exception of the fortress at Ochakiv, was ceded to Russia. In 1783 the unresolved question of control over Crimea, however, would lead Russia to formally annex the peninsula and adjoining steppes to the north and east along the Sea of Azov. All that remained of Ottoman

J. von Reilly, *Des Fürstenhums Moldau Noerdliche Hælfte* (1789)

J. von Reilly, *Des Fürstenhums Moldau Sudliche Hælfte* (1789)

J. von Reilly, *Die Landschaft Bessarabien* (1789)

J. von Reilly, *Die Ostchakowische Tartarey oder Westliches Nogaj auch Jedisan* (1789) rule in Ukraine were the Black Sea lowlands to the west between the Dnister and Boh Rivers, as well as Bessarabia. In a desperate effort to reclaim authority over Crimea, Ottoman Turkey would declare war on the Russian Empire in 1787. The defeat of Turkish forces in a number of important engagements on both land and sea resulted in a treaty of peace concluded at Iasi (1791). The terms of the treaty saw the Porte cede Ochakiv, the Black Sea territory between the Boh and Dnister, and territory in Kuban. It further renounced all claims to Crimea, effectively ending the Ottoman presence and firmly establishing Russia's authority over the Black Sea steppes in Ukraine.

The maps of the region produced in the last decade of the eighteenth century were relatively accurate. The technical aspects of mapping had been mastered by this time, but more directly, there was now a surplus of information surfacing from various sources. In 1789 Joseph von Reilly, a Viennese art dealer turned map publisher, would produce his highly successful *Shauplatz der fünf Thiele der Welt*, relying, for example, on Turkish accounts for place-names in the Black Sea lowlands. In an atlas of exceptional quality and elegance, von Reilly's maps contained historical references to the Russo-Turkish wars of 1739–45 and 1769–74, as well as to several decisive battles in the war of 1787–91 (Ochakiv, Iasi, Bendery, Khotyn), the outcome of which, significantly, had yet to be determined at the time of publication. Von Reilly's decision to produce an account of the war in progress points to the inquisitive nature of a public much interested in developments that had strategic implications for Europe and for France, Sweden, Prussia, and Austria-Hungary, in particular.

The handsome cartouches that grace the von Reilly maps follow the classical revival style that was in vogue in both republican and, still later, Napoleonic France. Increasingly favoured by the trade but also reflecting the pervasive role of war in the maturing state system, martial images would appear with greater frequency in the maps covering territory where recent battles had taken place, as in the case of the cartouche in von Reilly's map *Des Fürstenhums Moldau Sudliche Hælfte*.

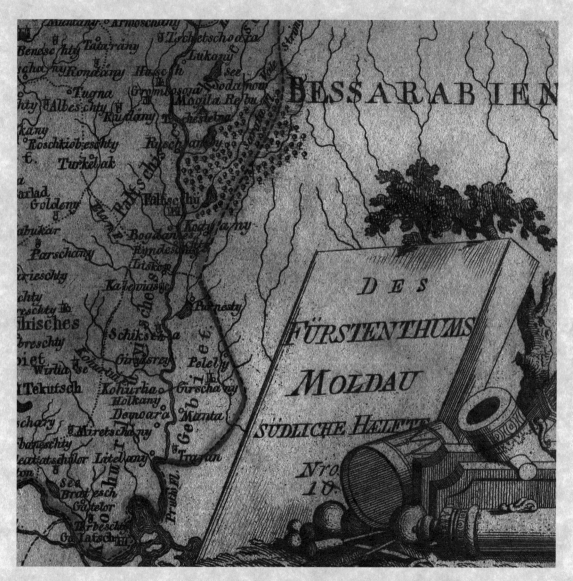

J. von Reilly, *Des Fürstenhums Moldau Sudliche Hælfte*, 1789 (detail)